HOOPS of STEEL

Lillenas Drama

Hicks & Cohagan's

HOOPS of STEEL

and Other Sketches

by
Stephen Hicks and Jerry Cohagan

Lillenas PUBLISHING COMPANY
KANSAS CITY, MO 64141

Stephen Hicks and Jerry Cohagan have coauthored six
sketchbooks with Lillenas. Along with their concert ap-
pearances, they have recorded four audiocassettes and
three videos, their newest concert video is titled *Hoops of
Steel*.

For more information regarding Hicks & Cohagan prod-
ucts or the performance ministry of Hicks & Cohagan,
please write to:

Hicks & Cohagan
P.O. Box 2894
Olathe, KS 66063
(913-631-6838 or 805-499-4306)

Cover art by Paul Franitza
Photos by J. E. Evans Studio

Printed in the United States of America

Contents

Preface

Can you believe it's been 13 years since our first collection of sketches was published by Lillenas? It's amazing what can happen when you combine the gift of stubbornness with a willingness to continue to annoy.

Truthfully, we are just as surprised as you that the performance ministry of Hicks & Cohagan has continued to flourish. We are constantly surprised at the fact that people will promote our performances or more courageously, perform our material themselves!

We would like to believe that over the years our skills as writers and performers have improved. (Or maybe we've just gotten more skilled at hiding our weaknesses . . .) Whether our craftmanship has improved or not, we do know that we are wiser and more thoughtful believers. Hopefully we are able to convey that in our writing.

We are also believers in drama and comedy with a Christian perspective. If this book is your first brush with the medium of live theatre, then hang on, you haven't seen anything yet! On the other hand, let us encourage you veterans. The changes we have seen in the quality of available material and the acceptance of drama in church settings is thrilling. Keep the faith.

Finally, let us issue our standard admonition and disclaimer. Use this material any way you can. If you can make it better, do it. Of course, if you perform the material and are a hit, we accept your gratitude. If it bombs, we stole these scripts from Custer & Hoose!

Under His mercy,
Stephen Hicks and Jerry Cohagan

Acknowledgments

As always, we owe a debt of gratitude to family and friends who with words and deeds continue to encourage us along the way. Special thanks to wonderful friends, Gary Bayer, Larry Campbell, Greg McNey, and Chaz Corzine.

Thanks to all our friends, old and new, who have proven the depth of the bond of friendship with acts of sacrifice and grace too numerous to recount.

Hoops of steel, dear friends, hoops of steel . . .

HOOPS OF STEEL

For some time, we have wanted to write about Christian relationships among men. Traditionally, it has been difficult for men to authentically communicate with each other, especially about things that matter.

But that is changing. As we encounter the various experiences life brings our way, we are beginning to understand that we really do need each other. Straight and true friends are rare and valuable. They may help us find meaning in some of life's most daunting circumstances. And they may help lighten the load with laughter. "Jeff" and "Greg" are learning the value of relationships forged in the fiery trials of life.

Playing Time:

10-12 minutes

Cast:

JEFF: *A genuine friend, concerned. Has a strong faith gained through experience. Late 30s to early 40s.*

GREG: *Life, at the moment, isn't all he thought it'd be. Bitter, yet honestly searching for God in the midst of his circumstance. Late 30s to early 40s, as well.*

Props:

Greg wears a tuxedo
Jeff is dressed in a suit and tie

Hoops of Steel

(As the scene opens we hear the Wedding Recessional. GREG walks onstage exhausted and sits in a pew next to JEFF, who has been watching all the action that is taking place out in front of them. The stained-glass window they refer to is played out over the audience. As GREG slumps in pew, the Wedding Recessional ends.)

JEFF *(pointing in front of him):* How many more pictures is that guy going to take?

GREG: I don't know. I left when he wanted a shot of the entire wedding party in the baptistery wearing snorkels and masks.

JEFF: Sounds like something from *People* magazine . . .

GREG *(wryly):* I still can't believe my little sister is finally married. Do you realize at her age she had a better chance of getting struck by lightning than catching a husband?

JEFF: Well, knowing your sister, Rob's the one who's going to think he got struck by lightning.

GREG *(ironic):* Are you suggesting Susan can be a little domineering?

JEFF: You heard the vows. He said "I do" to the preacher, then turned to her and said, "If that's OK with you, honey buns."

GREG: She can be a little forceful . . .

JEFF: I don't think he should've had to sign a prenuptial agreement in blood. Where'd they meet, anyway?

GREG *(sardonic):* At a "Single and Satisfied" conference.

JEFF: Makes perfect sense . . .

GREG *(stands to address imaginary little girl):* Amanda, honey? I think they want to see your face in the picture, so go ahead and put your dress down. That's right . . .

JEFF *(joining in, as well):* And go ahead and loosen little Michael's cummerbund. I know it's a wedding color, but his face shouldn't be purple.

GREG: And Michael, pull the ring bearer's pillow away from Amanda's face! Let her breathe . . .

JEFF: These photographs could end up as state's evidence.

GREG: Especially the one of me catching the wedding bouquet.

JEFF: I thought you told me the bouquet was for sissies. The garter was what real men catch.

GREG: Hey, I'm exploring my feminine side. Besides, I had a better shot at out-muscling those women. *(Sits back down)*

JEFF: That was quite a block you put on Aunt Louise. Her walker's the only thing that saved her.

GREG *(rubbing his shoulder):* Aunt Louise is no slouch.

JEFF: Yeah, she used that walker like it was a cow-catcher on the front of a train. I saw her barreling to the front of the line at the reception with that thing full of hats, purses, and umbrellas. Little Michael was trapped in there for an hour before somebody called 911.

GREG *(with a touch of bitterness):* Wouldn't be the first time a wedding was the scene of a crime, would it . . . ?

JEFF: Not exactly a Hallmark card sentiment, Greg.

GREG: Sorry I'm so cynical. I can't help it, weddings bring it out in me.

JEFF *(sits next to him, picking up on it):* Hey, I'm sorry to hear you and Lori are having some problems.

GREG *(dismissing it):* Yeah, me too. Everybody's sorry. Do you think I sound bitter enough?

JEFF: You're allowed a little of that.

GREG *(trying to lighten up):* Hey, I guess it's a good thing my sister and Rob didn't come to me for premarital counseling.

JEFF: I was a little concerned when you gave them a gift certificate to a law firm as a wedding present.

GREG *(bitter):* Wanted to be sure to get them something they could use.

JEFF *(attempting to console):* Seriously, if I can help you . . .

GREG *(stands, gesturing out in the sanctuary):* You wanna help, do something about these orange pews with mauve carpet. You think they meant to do that?

JEFF: Sure, they probably paid some consultant big bucks to tell them those colors were conducive to invitations.

GREG: Hey, I'd go forward if it meant not having to look at puce drapes.

JEFF *(stands):* Speaking of puce drapes, there goes Aunt Louise again. *(They both follow her with their heads across the audience in front of them, then both grimace.)* Wow . . . I think she took out three bridesmaids in one pass. How old is Aunt Louise, anyway?

GREG: Somewhere between 87 and the Second Coming. And just exactly whose aunt is she?

JEFF: Nobody knows. Forgive me for saying so, but with all she's been through, I'm kinda surprised she's still around.

GREG: Are you kidding me? She's like the Energizer bunny. She just keeps going and going and going. She offered me some great advice when Lori moved out. *(With an edge of mockery in his voice)* "Honey," she said. "If you wake up in the mornin' and you're still breathin', set your jaw, grit your teeth, quote a Bible verse, and don't ever look back. Doubt is a sure sign of weakness."

JEFF *(sits back down):* I used to believe that up until a few years ago. I thought that was the way God expected *real* men to handle things.

GREG *(gestures toward Aunt Louise):* Well, Aunt Louise is the most real "man" I know. And if it's worked for her all these years, it's good enough for me.

JEFF: You sure of that? I think maybe it's OK to struggle.

GREG *(glib, trying to appear jovial):* Hey, the struggle was trying to stay together. This is the easy part, waking up alone. *(Stops himself as the reality of what he's said hits him, then continues on, struggling)* You know, Lori and I stood at that very same altar *(points to it, out center)* . . . I remember the sun shining down through that stained-glass window, casting all these different colors on us. I believed that was a sure sign from God that this was meant to be. That there'd always be this piercing light of love shining on us . . . *(Looking up at window out over audience)* Now when I look up there, I just see a lot of broken glass.

JEFF: We all hurt at one time or another, Greg. It's OK.

GREG *(backing him off, gently):* You're not gonna make me listen to another Promise Keepers tape, are you, Jeff? I don't even think it's legal to have that much testosterone in one place at one time.

JEFF: All I'm saying is sometimes we can draw strength from knowing that we're not alone. That someone else has been down this road before. Nobody's life is perfect, and that's OK.

GREG *(mocking him):* "And that's OK." What is this, "Daily Affirmation" with Stuart Smalley? *(Dismissing his help)* Look, this is my life. Why should it matter to anyone else?

JEFF: I just know what it's like to feel that everything's been pulled out from under you.

GREG (a bit scornful): Yeah? Where'd you gain such great insight?

JEFF (takes a moment, then): Danny's death.

GREG (beat, then sits next to him): I'm sorry . . . You had that service right here, too, didn't you . . . ?

JEFF: Yeah . . . When I heard the thud of the lid closing on Danny's casket, I never thought I'd hear another sound. Joyce said it was like her heart stopped beating. Nothing but silence . . . no voices, no singing, no laughter, no God. Just anger, sadness, and pain. (Stands, remembering) Doesn't feel like four years ago. It feels like it could've been yesterday. When they lowered our son into the ground, I confess I wasn't thinking about how "all things work together for good for those who love the Lord and are called according to his purpose." There was no point, there was no purpose to any of it. Inside I was screaming, "Where are You! What have You done?" (Turns to GREG) I felt as lost as you do now. (Looks up at window) The only answer I ever got was that same light beaming through that window.

GREG (honestly hurting): Does it ever get any better?

JEFF: Sure. But it takes time and patience and a bit of endurance. And a lot of forgiveness.

GREG (crossing to JEFF): Look, I just don't want to end up like one of those guys on Oprah, you know . . . wanting somebody to hold his hand, and whining about how unfair life is and how "nobody knows the trouble I've seen" . . .

JEFF: Sometimes life is unfair. But I'm not sure I can count on Oprah to be there for me. Walking the path with real friends, knowing they've been there before . . . that's what gives me the strength to go on.

GREG: Maybe you're right . . .

JEFF (stares up at window, standing next to GREG): When I look at that window, I don't just see the broken pieces of your life or mine. I see old Mr. Henderson who buried his wife of 50 years last month . . . I think of the Winslows, whose teenage kid walked out of the house and never looked back . . .

(MUSIC UP—Reflective underscoring throughout remainder of sketch, if desired)

GREG (looking at window, as well): . . . the Kellys' finding out their only son has AIDS . . .

JEFF: Aunt Louise, a lonely lady whose scared of dying alone . . .

GREG: . . . my kids wondering what in the world's going on with Mommy and Daddy. Sometimes I wonder how any of us get through the day.

15

JEFF (*continuing to gaze at the window*): I'm not sure. There've been days the past four years when I didn't think I would. But life has a way of surprising you.

GREG: More like kicking you in the teeth. (*Steps forward, looking up at window*) You think Jesus ever "posed" for those paintings or stained-glass windows?

JEFF: I don't think He had the time. He was too busy making the journey with His friends.

GREG (*struggling*): So He knows what it's like . . . (*turning to* JEFF) even in the dark places?

JEFF (*puts a hand on* GREG's *shoulder*): Yeah, he knows. (*Looks up at window*) Greg, even in the dark, there's still that light. Maybe it takes all those broken pieces to see the real picture of God's love. (*Looks at* GREG) So if we share in the suffering, one day we'll share in the joy.

GREG (*looks at* JEFF): I hope so . . . I need that. Not much has turned out the way we thought it would, has it?

JEFF (*crosses back to pew and sits*): Did you ever think it would get easier as we got older?

GREG (*joining him*): Sure, everybody does. Our folks never told us it didn't. It's like this practical joke each generation plays on the next.

JEFF: Maybe you should've told your sister. I wonder where their journey will take them?

GREG: Nowhere for a while. (JEFF *looks at* GREG.) I let all the air out of Rob's tires. I figure they waited this long, what's another hour or two in the grand scheme of things?

JEFF (*laughs, then naively*): My, oh my . . . I wonder where you ever got such an idea?

GREG: I wonder. (*They chuckle, then*) But if I'd known what lay ahead, I might not ever have left the choir room for that altar. (*With genuine optimism*) But I think Lori and I'll make it.

JEFF: Blissful optimism?

GREG: No, my friend. (*Looks at window*) Hope. Real hope. (*Turns to* JEFF) What was it your dad said at our wedding? Something about the flowers?

JEFF (*remembering*): He said . . . that like those flowers, friends have to walk through endless winters and dark nights. But if you hold on, just like spring, light and joy will come again.

GREG: That's it. I hope that's true for Lori and me. Then you threw in some Shakespeare quote at our reception.

JEFF *(surprised):* You remember that?

GREG: Yes, I do. *(Looking out, recalling)* "The friends you have, whose lives are true and faithful; clutch them to your heart with hoops of steel." And anything is possible. *(Looks at* JEFF) Close?

JEFF: On the money. *(Putting an arm around* GREG) Hoops of steel, my friend . . . hoops of steel.

(Both gaze up at the stained-glass window, which briefly bathes them in colored light, then fades as music ends.)

HYMNS, PSALMS, AND MISDEMEANORS

(This sketch originally appeared in a slightly altered form as "The Bulletin Police" in volume 11 of the Worship Drama Library.)

This sketch is a lot of fun to do! After all, who wouldn't want to do their best Jack Webb character? It takes a gentle look at some of the nonessentials that can divide the body of believers.

It also pokes lighthearted fun along the way at the difference between what is sacred and what is a sacred cow. There are essential issues that we may not all agree on, but we believe that essentially God is creative and allows us to express ourselves in worship creatively, as well.

Playing Time:

5-7 minutes

Cast:

WALTER BEALS: *A mild-mannered average guy, a bit of a wimp. OK, he's a wet noodle.*
FRANK STEEL: *À la Jack Webb from "Dragnet," he's from the old school when it comes to interrogation technique.*

Props:

A remote control
One rumpled trenchcoat and hat
A worship bulletin, attendance card, and penlight

Hymns, Psalms, and Misdemeanors

(*Scene opens with* WALTER *slumped on a couch, flipping through the channels on imaginary TV in front of him.*)

WALTER (*couch potato, flipping remote on each choice*): Whadda we got here . . . Thighmaster . . . Thighmaster . . . evangelist with bad hair . . . evangelist's *wife* with bad hair . . . Psychic Friends Network, somehow I just knew it would be that. (*Doorbell rings,* WALTER *yells to imaginary wife offstage.*) I'll get it, Honey! You stay there with the macramé. (*Starts to cross stage left toward door*)

STEEL: Stay where you are, Sir! (WALTER *yelps in fear as he instinctively spins around with his hands in the air. He is greeted with the sight of* FRANK STEEL, *who has appeared from behind the couch. He wears a trenchcoat with the collar pulled up. He takes his job very seriously, and his face remains deadpan throughout. All his lines are delivered with very little inflection, almost monotone. His hand is in his pocket pointing a gun at* WALTER.) Mr. Walter Beals?

WALTER (*stunned*): Yes . . . ?

STEEL: Frank Steel. I'd like to ask you a few questions.

WALTER: But how'd you get in . . . ?

STEEL (*matter-of-fact*): I could tell you, but then I'd have to kill you. (*Gestures with gun hand for* WALTER *to sit back down on the couch*) Have a seat, Sir. (WALTER *quickly and meekly sits, bewildered.* STEEL *whips his gun hand out and shoves it in* WALTER's *face.*)

WALTER (*screaming, expecting a gun*): AHHH!

STEEL (*holding out a crumpled piece of paper*): You know what this is?

WALTER (*slowly looks, then unfolds it*): A church bulletin?

STEEL (*yanking it back, pacing*): That's right, Mr. Beals. A church bulletin—an order of service; a blueprint, if you will, to building the Kingdom; a road map to the noon buffet, a Rand McNally for worshipers. (*In his face*) You know what happens when you don't follow the map? You know what happens when you take a detour off the main interstate? Anarchy, Mr. Beals. You get anarchy.

WALTER *(meekly)*: Are you from Triple A?

STEEL: No, Sir. I'm not Triple A. I'm B.P.

(We hear the first four notes of "Dragnet"—"Dum, Da, Dum, Dum")

WALTER: B.P.?

STEEL *(deadpan straight ahead)*: Bulletin Police.

(We hear the last five notes of the "Dragnet" theme—"Dum, Da, Dum, Dum, Dummm.")

STEEL *(continues)*: We're an internal organization founded to protect the order of the church service and to monitor any underground activity or dissident behavior.

WALTER: You're kidding?

STEEL *(eyeballing him)*: No, Sir. I don't kid.

WALTER: Is this some kind of joke?

STEEL *(eyeballing him)*: No, Sir. I don't joke. *(Opening the church bulletin, begins to grill him)* On Sunday of last, did you or did you not participate in the responsive reading?

WALTER: I did.

STEEL: And at the end of said responsive reading were you or were you not heard to extemporize an "Amen"?

WALTER: Well, yes. But I was just—

STEEL *(flashing the bulletin in his face)*: Do you see the word "Amen" at the end of the responsive reading, Sir?

WALTER: Well no, but—

STEEL: Do you see any asterisk indicating a time for spontaneous outbursts?

WALTER *(stands)*: Now, just a minute here—

STEEL *(sits him back down)*: Sit down, Mr. Clap Happy. *(Paces about the stage)* That's how it starts, Mr. Beals. A little impromptu "Amen." Next thing you know, you got ad-libbed "Hallelujahs" cropping up all over the sanctuary. Pretty soon you got freewheeling testimonies. One thing leads to another, Mr. Agitator. One rabble-rousing crowd a year in the Easter pageant's enough.

WALTER: I didn't mean to start anything, I was just moved by the passage—

STEEL: If we wanted you to be moved, we wouldn't've padded the pews. (*Whips out an attendance card*) Know what this is?

WALTER: It's an attendance card.

STEEL: Bingo, Sherlock. (*Pointing to it*) That your signature?

WALTER: Could be . . .

STEEL: What's that say on the back?

WALTER: It's a note to the pastoral staff.

STEEL: Read it, Mr. "Rebel Without a Cause."

WALTER (*trying to justify*): It was just a suggestion.

STEEL (*shining a small penlight in his face*): This is a three-way bulb, buddy boy. Don't make me turn up the heat!

WALTER (*wilting under the pressure, reads*): "How 'bout some choruses along with the hymns?"

STEEL (*snatching card back and flourishing it above his head*): Aha! The smoking gun, Mr. Chorus Man.

WALTER (*breaking down, pleading his defense*): It was just an idea! I didn't really mean it!

STEEL: Sure you didn't, Mr. "Transparencies on an Overhead Projector," Mr. "Let's Just Praise the Lord"! It's not enough you feel compelled to clap during the singing, but you gotta do it on the offbeats. Not the two and four, like normal people, but the one and three! (*Shoving the bulletin under his blubbering nose*) What's that say!

WALTER (*reading through his sobs*): "Congregational Hymn."

STEEL: That's right, Happy Hands. (*Putting the bulletin away*) We want spontaneous worship, we'll sing all six verses of "How Firm a Foundation."

WALTER: I'm sorry . . .

STEEL: And another thing. During the hymns, let's keep those hands holstered. (*Illustrates his point with his hands*) There's an unwritten law that if you gotta raise your hands in order to sing, they better not go any higher than the pastor's sermon is long. (STEEL *holds his hands about a foot apart.* WALTER *meekly reaches over and pulls one of* STEEL's *arms further out, widening the gap and making the point that his pastor is a bit long-winded.*) Any further, and you got the makings of an insurrection. You got that, Joy Boy?

WALTER: Yes, Sir.

STEEL: And from now on, no more insurgent outbursts on your part. If you feel so moved by the pastor's sermon, a simple head nod *(demonstrating)* is sufficient. Anything more is a breach of protocol.

WALTER *(quickly nodding head):* Yes, Sir.

STEEL: I like that. A quick learner. You seem like a nice man, Mr. Beals. I'd hate to see you come to a bad end. Remember, the church bulletin is your friend. You treat it right, it'll see you out by noon, or at this church 12:15. You start abusing it, you got dry pot roast. Any questions? *(Not giving* WALTER *a chance)* Good. *(He is directly behind* WALTER.) Remember, I know where you live. If I have to, I'll be back. *(Threateningly)* And I'll be all over you like a pastor during a building campaign! *(Slaps attendance card on* WALTER's *forehead and drops behind the couch as we hear the "Dragnet" theme once more.* WALTER *blubbers. Blackout.)*

THE TIE THAT BINDS

Years ago we tossed around ideas for a sketch that would illuminate some of the challenges of being a single adult in a "married" world. Sometimes, well-meaning family and friends can make it difficult for single adults to simply be themselves.

Of course, meeting the expectations of others can be a bit burdensome no matter what one's marital status may be. This sketch reminds us that God's dreams and plans for us are very personal and unique. Perhaps one of the best gifts we can give each other—married, single, or undecided—is the freedom to become all that God desires for us to be, without manipulation or oppressive expectations.

It's tricky enough to find one's own way in this world, without the loving concerns of Auntie Vi . . .

Playing Time:

5-7 minutes

Cast:

AUNTIE VI: *A plump, matronly woman with a genuine concern for her nephew's marital status.*

RICHARD: *An average guy in his late 20s or 30s. He loves his auntie and knows all about family responsibilities. Sometimes the "ties that bind" can make it hard to breathe!*

Props:

Various cooking utensils, apron

The Tie That Binds

(As scene begins, AUNTIE VI *is bustling about in her kitchen busily mixing up some homemade goodie. Humming to herself, she is unaware of her nephew* RICHARD, *who enters.)*

RICHARD: Hi, Auntie Vi. I let myself in.

AUNTIE VI *(startled, she turns to him):* Mercy sakes alive! Don't ever sneak up on me like that. *(Clutching her heart)* You trying to rush me on to that great potluck in the sky?

RICHARD: Sorry, Auntie Vi. I didn't realize your health was so grave.

AUNTIE VI: Don't say "grave" to an old person!

RICHARD: Sorry I brought it up. *(Smiling at his lame joke)* Let's just lay it all to rest.

AUNTIE VI *(beat):* Just couldn't resist, could you?

RICHARD: Sorry. I just came by to check up on you.

AUNTIE VI: It's your lucky day. I'm just about to take my famous anchovy, cabbage, and prune casserole out of the oven.

RICHARD *(starting to leave):* Wish I could stay . . .

AUNTIE VI *(bending over at stove):* Goodness gracious! Somebody forgot to turn on the stove.

RICHARD *(looks heavenward and mouths "Thank you," then to* AUNTIE VI): That's all right. I'm on a strict nonanchovy, cabbage, and prune casserole diet.

AUNTIE VI: Well, you need to keep your health up. Look at you . . . *(Pokes him a couple places while "tsk, tsk"ing)* All skin and bones. You need to stay in shape for all those attractive bachelorettes.

RICHARD: "Bachelorettes"? Auntie Vi, you gotta stop watching those reruns of "The Dating Game."

AUNTIE VI *(not listening):* Say, I thought you were going to bring that little girlfriend of yours by? What was her name? Secretia . . . Lucretia?

RICHARD (*a bit resigned at this*): Lucy, her name was Lucy. Lucy Rogers. We had a little parting of the ways . . .

AUNTIE VI (*trying to recall*): Rogers . . . Not the Rogers who own all those computer stores? (*Concerned*) You didn't let one of them slip through your fingers, did you?

RICHARD: Sorry, Auntie Vi. I guess the relationship was terminal. I had to pull the plug. (*Enjoying his wit*) Get it? Computers, terminal? Pull the plug?

AUNTIE VI (*deadpan*): She died?

RICHARD (*sighing*): No, Auntie Vi, she didn't die. It just wasn't working out. Besides, these Rogerses ran a funeral home for pets. Their slogan was "Pet Paradise, from cat to canine we can either crate or cream 'em."

AUNTIE VI: Don't be disgusting. (*Sighs*) Lord knows your mother and I have tried to help you find someone . . .

RICHARD: Now don't start, Auntie Vi—

AUNTIE VI: It's a lonely world.

RICHARD: Please, Auntie Vi—

AUNTIE VI (*not listening*): How hard could it be to grant your dear old aunt one final wish?

RICHARD: Don't say it, Auntie Vi!

AUNTIE VI: Why don't you—

BOTH TOGETHER: Get married and settle down!

RICHARD: I knew it. You can't go a day without bringing that up. Did Mom put you up to it?

AUNTIE VI: We're just concerned, that's all—

RICHARD: She *did* put you up to it!

AUNTIE VI: We only want the best for you, Richie. Aren't there any nice girls at work?

RICHARD: Auntie Vi. I work for a collection agency. In my business, a nice girl is someone who doesn't meet you at the door with a blowtorch and a stun gun.

AUNTIE VI: What about church?

RICHARD: You kidding? The Sunday School classes are called "Pairs and Spares." Sure, there are some nice girls. But you can't ask anyone out without it ending up in the church newsletter.

AUNTIE VI: Don't exaggerate, Richie.

RICHARD: Before you know it, people are asking you if you have a favorite color of Tupperware.

AUNTIE VI: People just want you to be happy. Your Uncle Harold and I had 43 wonderful years together. You don't hear him complaining.

RICHARD: That's because Uncle Harold's been dead for 9 years.

AUNTIE VI *(to herself)*: I guess that means it wasn't him who lost the remote control. . . . What about children? Don't you want someone to carry on the family name?

RICHARD: Why would I want anyone to carry on the name Belchenfarger?

AUNTIE VI: Well, you know how much your mother wants grandchildren.

RICHARD: If she wants grandchildren so much, maybe I'll just find a girl and—

AUNTIE VI *(brandishing a spatula at him)*: Don't even think about it, Buster!

RICHARD: Just joking, Auntie Vi.

AUNTIE VI: Don't kid me. I know what you single guys think about! Between game shows, I watch them soap operas.

RICHARD: What on earth? *(Dawning on him)* Oh, I see, you mean—

AUNTIE VI *(covers her ears)*: Don't say it!

RICHARD: Sex.

AUNTIE VI *(grabbing her heart)*: Land o'Goshen, you said it.

RICHARD: Sure, it's a natural part of life.

AUNTIE VI *(brandishing a wooden spoon this time)*: Don't try to be "hip" with me, Sonny.

RICHARD: Auntie Vi, I know that there are certain aspects of a physical relationship that are sacred in marriage. I know that married couples do more than watch "Wheel of Fortune" when they're alone.

AUNTIE VI *(recalling, in her own world)*: I wish somebody would've told Harold.

RICHARD: What's that?

AUNTIE VI *(back to reality)*: Never mind. Don't be trying to get out of this by sounding mature, young man!

RICHARD: Look, I appreciate everybody wanting me to be happy. But I can't meet everybody's expectations. I don't plan to wear a button all my life that says "I'm single and proud of it!" And I'm not too thrilled to keep running into newlyweds who give me that "you don't know what you're missing" look, giggle, then skip off hand in hand. I just want to be myself.

AUNTIE VI *(missing her dig at him):* Why aim so low? Don't you think you'll be a better Christian if you're married?

RICHARD: Don't be silly, Auntie Vi. Look at all the single adults who were leaders in the Bible. If you want to get picky, look at what happened to Job; he was married! If God's plan for me includes marriage, great. If not, great. Either way, I know He loves me. And I am a complete person.

AUNTIE VI: Well, I guess you're right. I ought to trust God to take care of things. Sometimes I just want to help Him along.

RICHARD: And trust me, Auntie Vi. Believe it or not, I'm all grown-up.

AUNTIE VI *(moving toward him for a bear hug):* Not too grown-up for a hug, are you?

RICHARD *(attempts to hug her while she wraps him up and bodily lifts and hugs him):* Listen, I've got to go. I've got to stop by the grocery store and buy some Campbell's soup-for-one!

AUNTIE VI *(putting him down):* Smart aleck. Are you sure you can't stay for some Spam surprise?

RICHARD *(starting to leave):* I'd love to, but I've gotta run. Love you.

AUNTIE VI: I love you too. I'm glad we had this talk. *(Following him out)* Say, what about the Finklemeyer girl?

RICHARD: Are you kidding? She's built like a bowling alley.

AUNTIE VI *(excited):* I know, that's where I saw her! Bowled a 225, has her own ball. She's just your type. You can trust a girl who bowls . . .

RICHARD *(shaking his head and sighing):* Yes, Auntie Vi . . . *(They exit.)*

HOPELESS IN SEATTLE

Actually, we got this idea from a pastor at the Moody Bible Institute's annual pastors' conference. He was a "biker" pastor—no kidding! He had the leather jacket, beard, Harley Davidson, and a great idea for a sketch. As he talked about the undo pressures put upon pastors by their congregation, we began to see the makings of a clever sketch. OK, maybe it's not all that clever.

But the reality of stress and anxiety in this life is pretty much a given. It seems that the church should have an edge in dealing with such pressures. But sometimes we who have the answer only escalate the problem.

This is a lighthearted look at the angst that comes with church life. It's also a reminder to be thankful for your pastor . . . and to pray for him!

Playing Time:

7-9 minutes

Cast:

CALLER: *A stressed-out, haggard church layman who is on the edge. In this case, it's the edge of a window.*

PASTOR: *A suave, smooth, successful pastor who quickly unravels as his anxiety level rises.*

Props:

Two cellular phones
Legal pad and pen

Hopeless in Seattle

(Scene opens with anonymous CALLER *standing stage right on an imaginary window ledge facing the audience. He is desperate, obviously stressed out and pushed to his limits. He is looking down, surveying the street below. He closes his eyes and prepares to jump, then freezes in fear. After a brief moment he takes a cellular phone out of his pocket and dials a number. Phone rings stage left where our* PASTOR *is sitting at a desk diligently scribbling something down. He urgently reaches inside his suitcoat and pulls out another cellular phone.)*

PASTOR *(answering):* Crisis Intervention Hotline!

CALLER: Hello, I—

PASTOR *(interrupting immediately):* Hold please—*(Lays phone down and finishes writing something on pad at his desk)*

CALLER: What . . . ? Hello! . . . Anybody there?

PASTOR *(picking phone back up):* Yes, I'm here. Sorry, just had a thought for Sunday's sermon that didn't come from a Chuck Swindoll book. *(À la "Frazier" show)* Go ahead, I'm listening . . .

CALLER: I can't take it anymore! I mean it. I'm gonna jump!

PASTOR: No, wait! I'm here to help. Tell me your name.

CALLER: I can't do that. I'd prefer to remain anonymous.

PASTOR *(up on his feet, pacing):* Wouldn't we all. That's no problem, though. This nondenominational Crisis Hotline was set up to serve the entire Northwest. Believe me, with the weather up here we get the business. I had to convince a half-a-dozen callers last week that fiery orb in the sky wasn't the Second Coming—just the sun.

CALLER: I wondered about that . . .

PASTOR: And don't get me started on caffé latte overdoses. Anyway, to protect the anonymity of both the caller and the callee, your call was arbitrarily routed to one of 500 church offices somewhere in the Northwest. *(Pleased with himself)* Pretty slick, huh?

CALLER: Sure, whatever . . .

PASTOR: But what should I call you? Just anything, so it's a bit more personal?

CALLER *(in anguish):* I don't care what you call me! I give up! I'm at the end of my rope!

PASTOR: You sound pretty hopeless.

CALLER: I am!

PASTOR *(getting an idea):* How 'bout if I call you Hopeless! That all right?

CALLER *(considering):* Yeah, I guess. Whatever . . .

PASTOR *(pleased with himself):* All right, then. Hopeless it is . . .

CALLER: What about you, who am I talkin' to?

PASTOR: You know I can't divulge that. Let's just say I pastor an upwardly mobile congregation with seeker-sensitive services offering a variety of worship styles in a user-friendly facility. Including outreach services at the lake, we run well over a 1,000, even in the summer.

CALLER: Sounds nice . . .

PASTOR: Especially in a mission field like the Northwest. If Jesus had lived here, He would have had only six disciples. And you . . . ?

CALLER *(grimacing):* Well besides being in charge of Sunday School, I've just been voted a lifetime member of the church board.

PASTOR: Ouch!

CALLER: Tell me about it! Listen, I don't know why I called. There's nothing you can do. I'm wastin' your time . . .

PASTOR *(urgently):* No! Don't hang up! It can't be all that bad, Hopeless.

CALLER *(blubbering):* You just don't get it! I don't know why I'm talkin' to you. *(Defensive)* I've never used this number before . . . !

PASTOR: Of course not.

CALLER: It's just that this last week has pushed me over the edge! Our church is a mess. Our music director makes Al Gore look charismatic. And our choir! They refuse to be bound by things like notes and rhythm. And they wanted me to oversee the church finances. Our books make Whitewater look like grade school arithmetic. I'm jumpin'—here goes!

PASTOR: Wait! Don't jump yet! Tell me, where are you?

CALLER: I'm outside the church office. I crawled through a window.

PASTOR: You're on the ledge?

CALLER: You bet I am! . . . *(Looks down)* Well, more like a stoop, actually.

PASTOR: A stoop?

CALLER: Yeah, well, the office is on the first floor, but it's a start! I told ya I'd never done this before. Of course, the pastor's got a second-story office. *(Sarcastic)* Rev. "I'll pack a 5-minute devotional into a 30-minute sermon." Oh yeah, he's got the private bath, built-in shelves, a mahogany desk. I'm stuck in a closet marked janitorial supplies next to the cappuccino machine!

PASTOR *(digressing again)*: Is that the kind with the whipped cream attachment?

CALLER: That's it.

PASTOR: No matter how bad it seems, Hopeless, it isn't. Take me, for instance. You'd think I had it made. But it's amazing what a church board can do for your self-concept. My board meeting is the one place I can totally relax.

CALLER: Why's that?

PASTOR: It's the one place I know for certain I'm not in charge.

CALLER: Sounds rough.

PASTOR: Rough? We had to call in a UN negotiator just to change the size of the bulletin. And I've got a Sunday School superintendent that wants to eliminate Sunday School!

CALLER: How'd he get elected?

PASTOR: Are you kidding? That was his campaign slogan—"Elect Fred and Sunday School's dead!" The whole congregation chants it instead of the Doxology. Instead of tithe, I get little notes in the offering plate critiquing everything from the color of my socks to the part in my toupee. Instead of a place for sermon notes on the back of the bulletin they're starting to grade my sermons like Olympic gymnasts. Last week I scored lower than the teen's slide presentation of their work and witness trip to Mexico. *(Bitter)* Outpointed by a youth pastor in a sombrero doing the flamenco . . .

CALLER: You have to admit, it sounds entertaining.

PASTOR: What do you know? Balancing the books—it should be so simple. I'm like the activities director at summer camp. Senior adult ministries, single adult ministries, children's ministries, outreach ministries, men's programs, women's programs, youth programs, recovery ministries, Vacation Bible School, counseling ministries, marriage enrichments—and nobody is happy. I don't know why I even try sometimes.

CALLER: It can't be all that hopeless . . .

PASTOR: What do you know? That's pretty ironic coming from a guy who's just one step ahead of me. *(Breaking down)* Why do I even get up in the morning? I can't go on.

CALLER *(trying to encourage):* Sure you can. Listen, no matter what you're going through, there's still hope.

PASTOR *(full of angst):* No, it's hopeless.

CALLER *(quickly correcting him):* No, *I'm* hopeless.

PASTOR: Whatever.

CALLER *(sincerely):* And I'm here for ya.

PASTOR: A lot of good that does me. Look where you are. I couldn't even help you.

CALLER: Sure you did. After hearing what a mess your church is in, I feel a lot better. I think I can go on now.

PASTOR: Swell. Well, I can't. I've had it! I can't take any more of this! I'm jumping! *(Leaps up on top of his desk)* If it's good enough for you, then it's good enough for me! *(Steps forward to edge of his desk downstage and pulls open an imaginary window)*

CALLER: No! Don't do this!

PASTOR *(yelling both into the phone and out the window):* I can't go on pretending everything's all right! *(Screams, throwing up his arms in despair)* Aaagh!

CALLER *(in unison with the PASTOR's scream):* Noooo!

(Their screams eventually run out of steam, and they both stand there breathless for a moment. After a beat, the CALLER glances up to his left and stares at PASTOR. After a beat, he says into the phone . . .)

CALLER: Pastor Williams?

PASTOR *(looks down and to his right at CALLER, after a moment into the phone):* Fred? Is that you?

CALLER *(feebly lifts his hand in acknowledgment):* I didn't know you wore a rug.

PASTOR *(trying to lighten the awkwardness of the moment):* Tell you what, you don't mention my hairpiece to anyone and I'll trade you offices.

CALLER: Sounds good . . .

PASTOR *(trying to justify):* I wasn't really gonna jump, ya know . . . I was just trying to empathize.

CALLER *(joining in, as well):* Me neither! Everything's fine, I was just trying out the phone. You know, making sure the battery was charged.

PASTOR: Oh, of course, of course.

CALLER *(checking his watch):* Well, I better get ready for board meeting.

PASTOR: Me too. I've got to present my report on the seven steps of stress-free management.

CALLER: Right. And I've got the devotional. I'm calling it "Living on the Edge." See you inside.

PASTOR: Right.

(They both put their phones back in their pockets. CALLER starts to step back through his window while the PASTOR starts to close his. CALLER stops and looks up.)

CALLER: Uhh, Pastor Williams . . . ?

PASTOR *(looking down):* Yeah, Fred?

CALLER: Isn't tonight the meeting when we vote on the debt reduction plan for the new year?

PASTOR: I believe it is.

(Both simultaneously turn and look out at audience, throw their hands up in the air as if jumping, and scream.)

BOTH: Aaaaaaaaaaagh! *(Blackout)*

HOME IMPROVEMENT

As we have gotten older, we have realized the changing nature of human relationships. Nothing much stays the same. Especially relationships between sons and dads. We hope "Home Improvement" offers a glimpse of a son honoring his father and assuming new responsibility. And the image of a father acknowledging the passage of time and its effect on his role as the all-wise, all-knowing head of the family.

We hope this sketch shows the challenges of letting go of expectations we may have for ourselves and those we love. And also the new dimensions of love and honor that may take their place. Oh yeah, and we think some of this stuff is funny too! And it's a chance to play with tools.

Playing Time:

10-12 minutes

Cast:

SON: *In his 40s, realizing the responsibility that comes with being a son.*

DAD: *In his late 60s or early 70s, a bit gruff, used to being in charge, scared to grow old.*

Props:

A small, wooden box

Post-it notes

Hammer, flathead screwdriver, Phillips screwdriver, pliers, wrench

Home Improvement

(DAD *and* SON *are at a workbench in the garage.* DAD *is building some type of small box the size of a loaf of bread while* SON *is trying to appear helpful. There are various tools laid out neatly on the workbench.*)

DAD: Hand me that dohickey there.

SON: The what?

DAD: You know, that whatchamacallit . . .

SON (*holds up hammer*): This whatchamacallit?

DAD: Not that, the thingamajabber there!

SON (*holds up pliers*): This?

DAD: No, the flibberty gadget by your arm . . .

SON: Which one?

DAD: Your left arm!

SON: Not which arm, which flibberty gadget?

DAD: The one with the dohickey by it!

SON (*holding up pliers*): I thought this *was* the dohickey!

DAD: No, Son. That's the thingamabob. I'm asking for the flibberty gadget next to the dohickey. Now are you gonna hand it to me or not?

SON (*holds up Phillips head screwdriver*): You mean this?

DAD: Of course, that! Don't you listen anymore?

SON: Why didn't you just say Phillips head?

DAD: You're so smart, why didn't you just hand it to me in the first place! My son, 40 years old and he still doesn't know his dohickey from his thinga-mabob . . . what a nincompoop.

SON: Dad, if there's one thing you've taught me it's using tools. "You want a job done right, you use the right tool for the right job." Now, how come you didn't just ask me for the Phillips head?

DAD: I guess I figured after 40 years, you'd know what I needed without me telling ya.

SON: I'm not a mind reader, Dad.

DAD: Well, at my age there ain't that much to read. 'Sides, I've got everything labeled there.

SON: Where?

DAD: Right there, along the side.

(SON *notices Post-it notes stuck along the side of the workbench.*)

DAD *(continues):* See. *(Holds up pliers)* Thingamabob—*(Holds up hammer)* Dohickey—*(Holds up flathead screwdriver)* Whatchamacallit—*(Holds up wrench)* Thingamajabber and—*(Holds up Phillips head screwdriver)* Flibberty gadget!

SON *(holds up hammer):* This is a thingamajabber?

DAD: No, that's the dohickey.

SON *(holds up pliers):* I thought this was the dohickey.

DAD: No, that's the thingamabob.

SON: Then what's the thingamajabber?

DAD *(holds up wrench):* This is.

SON: I thought that was the whatchamacallit!

DAD: No—*(Holds up flathead screwdriver)* This is the whatchamacallit.

SON *(takes flathead screwdriver):* This is the whatchamacallit?

DAD: Correct.

SON *(picks up hammer):* Then that makes this a dohickey.

DAD: Yes . . .

SON *(picks up wrench and pliers):* And these are the thingamajabber and the thingamabob!

DAD *(holds up the Phillips head screwdriver):* Which brings us back to the flibberty gadget!

SON: How do you remember all that?

DAD *(as if to a simpleton):* 'Cause it's labeled!

SON: Wait a minute. Why don't you just label the flibberty gadget a Phillips head, the thingamabob pliers, the whatchamacallit a flathead screwdriver, the thingamajabber a wrench, and the dohickey a hammer?

DAD: 'Cause I can't remember that. Don't you see, I'm starting to forget everything I've known all my life. It's easier for me to learn something new than to try and remember what I already know . . . which I forget.

SON: I give up. You talk like you're as old as Methuselah.

DAD: Well, birthdays make me feel it. I've gotten a year older since the last one, ya know.

SON: Well, you're not ancient.

DAD: No, but pretty close to antique. Hand me the whatchamacallit.

SON *(reaching for the screwdriver):* That'd be the flathead. Why did you start using Post-it notes?

DAD: It helps me remember.

SON: They're all over the house. When I went to brush my teeth this morning, there was a note on the tube that said, "Put the cap back on when done." I thought it was for me. I felt like I was six years old again.

DAD: That *was* for you. I don't brush my teeth anymore. I soak 'em in a glass.

SON: That wouldn't be the Tweety glass I got a drink out of this morning, would it?

DAD: The very same.

SON: Great. There wasn't any note on *that* glass.

DAD: Must've ran out.

SON: Well, I guess I know what to get you next year. A case of Post-it notes.

DAD: Couldn't hurt. Hand me the thingamabob.

SON *(figuring it out, hands pliers):* That'd be the pliers. When do you wanna go over to the church?

DAD: What for?

SON: To repair the bench. We talked about this last week on the phone, remember? You said the arm was coming loose on our bench by the gazebo, and I said we'd fix it when I came down this weekend.

DAD: Oh, yeah. Well, that isn't necessary now.

SON: Why?

DAD: It's been fixed.

SON: You did it without me? *(Hurt)* Dad, I've been looking forward to working with you on that bench all week.

DAD: Well, your mom and I weren't sure you'd be coming down.

SON: I told you I was.

DAD: Guess I forgot.

SON: You didn't forget, you just didn't want my help. Why?

DAD: No, I just forgot. That's all.

SON: Dad, you and I built that bench together when I was 14. It was *our* project.

DAD: I remember. I had to do something to keep you from runnin' with those McCaskill boys. That was a one-way road to a dead end, those boys.

SON: We weren't that bad, Dad.

DAD: Oh, I know! That's what you said to me at two in the morning when Officer Paxton brought you home in his squad car.

SON: All we did was steal some crab apples.

DAD: All you did was trespass and break out every streetlight on Main.

SON: I always did have a good arm. Anyway, we spent every Saturday for two months building that bench. We sanded that thing smoother than a baby's bottom.

DAD: It was one of the few things you'd still do with me.

SON: And it kept me close to the church.

DAD: And away from the McCaskill boys.

SON *(smiling):* I knew what you were doing.

DAD: You didn't seem to mind.

SON: I didn't. But I couldn't tell *you* that. After all, at 14 I certainly didn't need my dad looking out for me. At least, that's what I told the McCaskills. Whatever happened to those two guys, anyway?

DAD: One's the mayor and the other's chief of police.

SON: You're joking?

DAD *(missing the irony):* Nope, they got my vote. Good men, both of 'em.

SON *(shaking his head):* I don't know how you put up with me, Dad.

DAD: That bench was my way of staying close to you through that age. Boy, you were a headstrong kid.

SON: It's the gene pool, Dad.

DAD: But I knew you'd turn out all right. *(Looking at him)* Well, I wasn't far off.

SON: So why didn't you wait for me to help you? (DAD *shrugs.*) We've always kept that bench up together.

DAD: I don't know . . .

SON: Come on, Dad . . . what is it?

DAD: Maybe I didn't want you poking fun at my work habits. *(Holding up a tool)* I don't call everything by their proper name, ya know.

SON: Dad, I didn't mean anything by it . . .

DAD: Well, I guess if you really cared about that bench you'd check on it for yourself once in awhile. I can't always be the one to maintain it.

SON: What are you talking about—?

DAD *(becoming agitated)*: I mean, I'm not always gonna be around to fix things. I can't always be the one calling you every time there's a problem.

SON: Dad, calm down—

DAD: I'm just saying that there comes a time when *you* gotta do some things. If you care about the bench, then *you* take care of it! *(Throws hammer down on bench)*

SON *(putting his hand on his dad's)*: It's all right, Dad. I'm sorry . . .

DAD *(stepping away):* I didn't fix the bench.

SON: What do you mean?

DAD: I didn't fix the bench. I hired it done.

SON: What . . . why?

DAD: I loaded up my tools. I drove down to the church. I sat down on our bench and studied the loose arm. I opened up my toolbox . . . and I stared at them. I just stared at them. *(Looks up at* SON, *a bit at a loss)* I couldn't remember what anything was, I couldn't remember how to fix the arm, I couldn't remember what to use. I spent all morning sitting there trying to make myself remember! Don't you see . . . I couldn't *remember!* *(Taps his fist against his temple)* I *couldn't* fix the bench! I couldn't do it!—

SON *(going to* DAD, *taking his arm)*: It's OK. It's all right, Dad. It's all right. Don't worry . . .

DAD: It's just that, you see . . . I don't like this growing old. And I'm a bit scared.

SON: It's OK, Dad. It's all right—

DAD: It's hard to give up doing things. I don't like letting go . . .

SON: I know, Dad. Maybe you don't have to let go. You said it yourself, Dad, I'm 40 years old. Maybe it's time to let me do a bit more? Don't let go, Dad . . . just hang on to me for some things.

DAD: Yes, well . . . *(crossing back to workbench)* I'm sure your mom would like to see you a little more often.

SON *(giving him his dignity):* Yeah, I imagine she would.

DAD: She could certainly use your help around here. She's not nearly as organized as she used to be.

SON: Maybe she could use some Post-it notes?

DAD: Ha! That'd be the day. She's a stubborn woman, your mother. I don't know where she gets it from.

SON: Maybe it's like a virus? (DAD *looks at him.)* You hang around it enough, you're bound to catch it. *(Smiles at* DAD)

DAD *(beat, then smiles back):* Maybe . . . *(Holds up small box he has built)* Well, what do you think?

SON: The hole's a little small, isn't it?

DAD: Why?

SON: There's no way the mailman can get a letter in there.

DAD: It's not a mailbox. It's a birdhouse.

SON: Oh. It's very nice, Dad. Can I give it a try?

(DAD *hands* SON *the birdhouse.)*

SON: Hand me the hammer . . . (DAD *looks at tools, a bit lost.* SON *notices, then gently.)* I mean . . . the dohickey.

(DAD *looks up at* SON, SON *smiles and holds out his hand.* DAD *smiles, then hands* SON *the hammer.)*

DAD: Dohickey, it is—

SON *(smiles, then):* Whatchamacallit—

DAD *(placing it in his hand, just like assisting a surgeon):* Whatchamacallit—

SON: The thingamajabber—

DAD: Thingamajabber—

(Lights begin to fade on them, as they continue to smile and work together in tandem.)

SON: Flibberty gadget—

DAD: Flibberty gadget—

SON: Thingamabob—

DAD: Thingamabob—

(Darkness)

DOORBELL BLUES

There is no doubt we are called to live lives of compassionate generosity. But sometimes, the magnitude of the task before us can be overwhelming. It is easy to feel surrounded by apathy and selfishness. The cloak of self-righteousness and self-pity can be easy to wear when our efforts seem taken for granted or not rewarded.

With "Doorbell Blues" we want to remind folks that it's important to keep God's perspective on our mission. The sketch provides excellent opportunities for human-produced sound effects and quick character/costume changes. Big and broad is the order of the day.

Playing Time:

8-10 minutes

Cast:

PHILIP: *A bedraggled solicitor going door-to-door for worthy causes.*

COSMO: *A flaky guy who sees conspiracy all around him, not at all in touch with reality.*

VANNA: *A rather large, domineering woman, dressed in an ugly bathrobe and bunny slippers. About as opposite from Vanna White as possible.*

BURT: *A paranoid guy, we only see his eye peering through a crack behind his chained door.*

ANDREW: *A cheerful fellow who's a bit perky, but not to the point of being obnoxious.*

Props:

Various brochures for worthy causes

A wallet full of identification

A tin foil space helmet with antennae

Bathrobe and slippers

Production Note:

All sound effects for doorbell themes can be made by the various actors behind their respective doors. The doors themselves can, of course, be mimed.

Doorbell Blues

(PHILIP *enters carrying a variety of brochures and paraphernalia representing many charitable causes. He gathers himself together and approaches the first door. As he rings the doorbell the theme from "Close Encounters" is heard.* COSMO *spins around and opens the door.*)

PHILIP: Hello, sorry to bother you—

COSMO *(wearing a foil helmet with antennae, conspiratorially)*: Hey! Are you with the Company?

PHILIP *(taken aback)*: What company?

COSMO: You know, the Company, the Organization, the CIA.

PHILIP: No, of course not. I represent a variety of organizations who need your donation—

COSMO *(interrupting)*: Donation? What? A kidney, a lung, a heart?

PHILIP: A heart?

COSMO: Sure, whatever is needed. *(Conspiratorially)* Remember, the truth is Out There.

PHILIP *(not sure what he's dealing with)*: Sure it is . . . As I was saying, we're looking for folks who are willing to donate time and resources—

COSMO: What's the frequency, Kenneth?

PHILIP: What are you talking about?

COSMO *(grabbing his head)*: Hold it! I think I'm getting a message from Out There. *(Begins slapping his tin foil helmet)*

PHILIP: How about a message from right here?

COSMO: Yes, here it is! "Cowboys 17, Green Bay 10." *(To* PHILIP*)* Is that a code? What does it mean?

PHILIP: It means I lost 10 bucks.

COSMO *(conspiratorially)*: What?

43

PHILIP (smiling): Nothing. Just joking.

COSMO (with dire seriousness): It's no joke, buddy.

PHILIP (trying to steer the conversation back to earth): Of course not. But neither are the millions of people without basic—

COSMO (interrupting again): Cable? I can't believe it. A lifetime without Star Trek, the X-Files . . .

PHILIP (backing away): Look, maybe now isn't a good time . . .

COSMO: Now! Oh no, it started a long, long time ago in a galaxy far, far away . . . (Looks around conspiratorially, then slams door shut)

PHILIP (stepping away): Send me a postcard. (Shakes it off and regroups) How hard can this be? Be assertive, be direct, demand a response. After all, people want to help other people. You just gotta give 'em the opportunity. (Approaches the next door and rings doorbell. The "Jeopardy" theme is heard.)

VANNA (swinging open her door, she stands there in a bathrobe and slippers, domineering): Yeah, so wadda you want?

PHILIP (frightened, takes a breath and begins): Thank you so much for your time. I'm Philip Wasson (points to his name tag I.D. and then unfolds a long wallet inset). As you can see, I have been authorized to represent a number of charitable and worthy organizations—

VANNA (like spitting nails out of her mouth): Make it snappy, Phyllis, we're "Wheel" watchers.

PHILIP: Beg your pardon?

VANNA: "Wheel of Fortune"! With charming host Pat Sajak and the lovely Vanna White. (Aside) She's my namesake.

PHILIP (under his breath): Startling likeness—

VANNA (looking back inside her house, yelling at her husband): What? How many times have I told you, Edgar, don't touch the remote. I've got a new stun gun, and I'm not afraid to use it!

PHILIP (mutters): He'd probably be grateful.

VANNA (back to PHILIP): What? Anyway, Philbert, how much for the cookies?

PHILIP: I'm not selling cookies, I'm—

VANNA (cutting him off): Then why am I talking to you? (Looks back inside, yelling at the TV) Don't buy a vowel! It's old testament brothers, how hard can it be? (Thinking hard) Cain and . . . Arnold? Cain and . . . Alphonse?

PHILIP (a bit irritated): Abel, Cain and Abel.

VANNA: Have you seen this one before? 'Cause I got 'em all on tape, and I don't recall this one. Is this a repeat?

PHILIP: No, just had a hunch, I guess.

VANNA: So, when do I get the cookies?

PHILIP *(losing patience):* I'm not selling cookies!

VANNA *(leaning over him menacingly, grabbing him by the collar):* Watch it, Buster. I'm not afraid to use that stun gun. I'll flip you like a three-egg omelette, toss you like day-old Caesar salad, lay you out like shag carpet.

PHILIP *(meekly, with a squeaky voice):* I'll have the cookies next week.

VANNA *(releasing him):* That's more like it. *(Back yelling at the TV)* No! Don't buy the lamp for $2,000! *(Slams door shut)*

PHILIP *(straightening his collar, attempting to motivate himself):* OK, keep your spirits up. Project openness and honesty. *(Approaches the next door and rings the doorbell, we hear someone yell "Dead Man Walkin'."* PHILIP *looks around, shrugs his shoulders.)* Naw . . . couldn't be. *(Rings doorbell again, and again we hear "Dead Man Walkin'.")*

BURT *(from behind the door, very paranoid):* Who's out there? What do you want?

PHILIP: My name's Phil Wasson, World Compassion International. *(Pointing to his name tag I.D.)* I'd like to talk to you about—

BURT *(looking through peephole in door):* Just a minute. *(He begins a long process of undoing the locks on his door, of which there are half a dozen.* PHILIP *starts to speak a couple of times, thinking* BURT *is getting closer, only to be held back by another lock.* BURT *finally opens his door an inch and peers from behind the crack.)* Who are you?

PHILIP *(starts to unfold the wallet inset again, then stops):* I'm with—Oh, never mind.

BURT: How rude. That's the last time I open my home up to a stranger. *(Shuts door)*

PHILIP *(his spirits are sagging):* OK, so it's a little dry spell. One more door and I'm outta here. *(Approaches yet another door, rings the bell, and we hear the up-beat chorus "Tomorrow" from "Annie")*

ANDREW *(swings his door open wide, and smiles):* Hi there! Isn't it just a great day to be alive?

PHILIP *(warily):* It could be . . .

ANDREW *(with a perky smile):* I'd rather be here than the best hospital in town!

PHILIP *(pondering):* If I thought my insurance would cover it . . .

ANDREW: So, what can I do for you?

PHILIP: You don't want to contribute to a worthy cause, do you? No, of course not, sorry to take up your time. *(Turns to leave)*

ANDREW: Wait. I'm pretty busy, but I might be interested.

PHILIP *(stunned):* Really? *(Quickly unfolds his I.D.)*

ANDREW: Impressive.

PHILIP: It let's everyone know I'm serious about compassionate ministries.

ANDREW: I can see. Come on in.

PHILIP *(hesitating):* You sure? Strangers aren't very welcome these days.

ANDREW: I'll take my chances. Besides, Vanna sold me her old stun gun.

PHILIP: Well, thanks. *(Steps inside and sits down)* I'm Philip Wasson, World Compassion International.

ANDREW: I'm Andrew. Sounds impressive, Philip.

PHILIP: Actually, it's just me, an answering machine, and a Xerox at Kinko's.

ANDREW: Nonetheless, you're connected to some wonderful organizations. *(Thumbing through the brochures)*

PHILIP *(unburdening himself a bit):* Like anyone is interested. I spend most of my time showing people our tax returns, financial statements, letters of endorsement, donor lists, state licenses, mission statements, lawyer briefs—

ANDREW *(holding up his hands):* I get the picture. Still, you can't be too careful with your investments these days.

PHILIP: Oh sure, then I have to listen to every story or rumor about misspent donations or morally corrupt spiritual leaders.

ANDREW: Now that you mention it—

PHILIP *(interrupting him):* Don't start with me. I mean if people don't want to give, they should just admit it without looking for excuses to justify their selfishness.

ANDREW: And feel all that guilt?

PHILIP: OK, OK, I know there are some folks who can make you feel guilty for breathing the air, let alone for living in a country like ours. But maybe underneath that false guilt is real God-given conviction. *(Throwing up his hands)* Aww, what's it matter, anyway?

ANDREW: You sound like you're suffering from a case of compassion burnout.

PHILIP *(dejected):* Not a spark left, as if anyone cared.

ANDREW: At least you're making a difference.

PHILIP: Am I?

ANDREW: So you feel like you're not even making a dent in the problem? (PHILIP *nods his head.*) Not even a fender bender? (PHILIP *nods his head a bit more aggressively.*) Not even a ding? (PHILIP *vigorously nods.*) A slight scratch?

PHILIP: All right, I think you've covered it. What's the point? People don't care about people. *(Unloading)* And the people I'm supposed to help! Our halfway house for prisoners might as well have continuous shuttle service back to the prison for all the good it does. *(Stands up and starts pacing around, getting more and more agitated)* And feeding the world's hungry? Well, excuse me, but they live in a desert! What do they expect? Spontaneous plant growth? And by the way, while your children are going hungry, that's a cow walking through your living room! And maybe there'd be a few less refugees if they wouldn't start wars in the name of God. Maybe their country is in chaos because they keep killing people because they have the wrong last name!

ANDREW *(agreeing):* Sure, why should it be your job to feed the hungry?

PHILIP: That's right.

ANDREW: Let 'em clothe their own needy.

PHILIP: Exactly!

ANDREW: Why not let professionals deal with convicts and degenerates. Who wants to hang around with a bunch of losers?

PHILIP: My thoughts, exactly.

ANDREW: One person can only do so much. How come you have to carry the weight of the world's failures on your shoulders!

PHILIP: Right, I'm only one guy.

ANDREW: Let somebody else get serious about compassion. Who do they expect you to be—Jesus?

PHILIP: Exact—! *(Stops himself. Slowly it dawns on him.)* Well, He did say what I was doing for the least of humanity, I was doing for Him . . .

ANDREW: Sure He did. But use some common sense, be realistic.

PHILIP: But most folks around Him didn't think He was very realistic.

ANDREW: Isn't a good soul-winning campaign all that matters?

PHILIP: He did use meeting people's needs as a way to reveal God's grace and the depth of their need . . . *(Looks up at him;* ANDREW *smiles at him)* Hey, you're good.

ANDREW: I try. Let me see all this stuff. *(Takes all the brochures)* How hard can it be? *(Steps outside door to role-play, rings the doorbell, PHILIP launches into "Tomorrow.")* I've gotta change that song . . . tomorrow.

PHILIP *(opening the door, playing along):* What do you want?

ANDREW: Well, I—

PHILIP *(cutting him off):* Sorry, I'm burnt out! *(Slams the door, pleased with himself)*

ANDREW: Hey, wait a minute! I—*(Stops, considers the lesson for himself)* I guess it's time to get serious about this. After all, how tough can this be? *(Approaches the next door, rings bell, we hear "Dead Man Walkin'!" ANDREW looks out at audience. Blackout.)*

SIGNS OF THE TIMES

Folks have always been fascinated with the end times. Eschatology is a popular course of study for pastors and laypersons alike. It seems to us that an almost obsessive preoccupation with the last days can be a convenient way to avoid the practical responsibilities of following Jesus. We used "Signs of the Times" to poke a little fun at end times fanatics and skeptics. And to offer a gentle reminder about our true priorities.

Ideally, this sketch should be done in lighting suggesting a cave environment. The more props used to "set the scene," the better. This sketch offers opportunities for some creative physical business. Have fun!

Playing Time:

8 minutes

Cast:

PERRY: *A gung ho end times believer, he is a bit obsessed with knowing the exact time and date of the return of Jesus.*

RON: *More of less tagging along for the fun of it, a likable enough guy who can't resist taking potshots at Perry's obsession.*

Props:

Various charts and maps
Two flashlights, two hard hats
An old, dirty pizza coupon

Signs of the Times

(Two guys enter what appears to be a dark cave. They are wearing hard hats while carrying all types of exploring gear; flashlights, maps, charts, and so forth. PERRY leads the way, committed to the expedition, while RON, not quite so gung ho, follows a step or two behind.)

PERRY *(into the darkened, inky void in front of him):* Hellooo . . . We come in peace . . .

RON: We also come in darkness. This is a cave, Perry, not the final frontier.

PERRY *(mysteriously):* Who knows what we'll find or where it will lead?

RON: Hopefully to a port-a-john. I thought you said iced tea was a good replenisher for hiking.

PERRY *(correcting him):* We are not hiking, we are spelunking.

RON: That may be true if I don't find that port-a-john.

PERRY: Try to be more reverent. We're on a mission, a quest. *(Suddenly stops RON, shines his flashlight on the ground)* Look! Ancient remains!

RON *(lifts up his shoe, as if having stepped in something):* Not that ancient. *(Shines his flashlight on his shoe)* Bat guano. I don't know how I let you talk me into this end-times expedition. How urgent can this be? What exactly are we looking for?

PERRY: Our Sunday School teacher, Dr. Lawrence, suggested his research revealed that this cave might hold some hidden clues to the exact return of Jesus and the end of the world.

RON: That's exactly why I don't go to Sunday School. Dr. Larry is a veterinarian. What are we looking for—the four horsemen of the apocalypse?

PERRY *(shines light directly in RON's face):* Hey! This is very important information. I've used all the charts and maps available to come to this exact location.

RON: Perry, we are standing in a cave 150 yards behind a Pizza Hut. Where did you get your information, Paul's little-known epistle, the letter to the Pepperonians?

PERRY: Mock if you must. Sometimes meat toppings hold quite a few secrets. *(Studies the cave wall)*

RON: Yeah, like what they're made of. *(Begins entertaining himself by making shadow puppets)* Hey, look at this . . . the three wise men.

PERRY *(pulling down RON's hands)*: Cut that out! This is serious. I have devoted hours of intense study to this matter. I take a very scholarly approach.

RON: I don't think a complete video library of "Highway to Heaven" and Time-Life books "Mysteries of the Universe" is all that scholarly.

PERRY *(not really listening to RON)*: I can't help it. I'm hooked on eschatology. *(Delving deeper into the cave)*

RON: I think I know of a rehab clinic for you. They make you watch *A Thief in the Night* over and over.

PERRY *(picks up a dirty scrap of paper)*: Look!

RON: What?

PERRY: I've found something. It appears to be a piece of ancient manuscript written on papyrus! (PERRY *shines his flashlights on it,* RON *joins him.)* I can't quite make it out. It's either Hebrew or the original Aramaic!

RON *(taking piece of paper)*: Let me see that.

PERRY *(pointing)*: Right there! Can you read it?

RON *(squinting at paper)*: "Supreme . . ."

PERRY *(excited)*: "Supreme" . . . yes!

RON: "Supreme" . . . something or other.

PERRY *(imagination running wild)*: "Supreme—Supreme Being"!

RON: Followed by . . . "Prepare" something "way"—

PERRY *(filling in the blanks)*: "Prepare the way for the Supreme Being"!

RON: Then down here at the bottom it says, "Two . . . for . . . one . . ."

PERRY: "Two for one" . . . Obviously a biblical allusion to John's Book of Revelation! *(Attempting to make some type of quote)* "Two men going up a hill, one gets taken, one left standing still!"

RON: That's not John. That's Larry Norman.

PERRY *(caught up in his zealous excitement)*: I can't believe it! Do you know what this means!

RON *(still squinting at paper)*: Yeah, I think I do. I think it means we can get a "Supreme pizza prepared any way we want." This is a two for one coupon. (PERRY *visibly wilts at the news.* RON *suddenly exclaims and points.*) Wait a minute! Look!

PERRY *(looking over* RON's *shoulder):* What is it!

RON *(genuinely excited for the first time):* There's no expiration date. This is still good!

PERRY *(grabbing coupon from Ron, shoves it in his pocket):* This is all a joke to you, isn't it? Well, for some of us we are about making important discoveries.

RON: Like when you thought you'd found the Bible's missing book of prophecy?

PERRY: It was an honest mistake. Daniel could've had a lesser known brother named Ernest.

RON: This just seems like a lot of wasted energy to me.

PERRY *(smugly):* Well, you won't think so when I tell you that I have arrived at the definitive date for the end of the world.

RON: Again? I'm still trying to pay off my credit cards I ran up before the "last definitive date" you arrived at for the end of the world.

PERRY: Visa probably wasn't amused when you told them they could send the next bill to 777 Streets of Gold.

RON: They stopped laughing when I told them my grace period was eternity.

PERRY: *This* time I have combined my own extensive knowledge of current events and world news—

RON *(interrupting):* You're not going to bring up that computer in Germany again?

PERRY *(ignoring him):*—Along with Dr. Lawrence's extensive biblical research. He's read Revelation in both the original King James *and* the NIV. *(Plunging on)* I've fed all that information into my laptop and have come up with the exact hour and date. *(Looks at* RON *knowingly)*

RON *(beat, then):* All right, I'll bite. Just so I don't waste time on a calendar I don't need, are you going to give me a hint?

PERRY: Well . . . I wouldn't worry about buying Christmas gifts this year.

RON: Great! That means I won't have to eat Aunt Viola's flaming fajitas. The fireball last year didn't leave an unsinged eyebrow in the house.

PERRY: We have verified our prediction and narrowed it down to November 7 of this year, at precisely 6:30 P.M. eastern standard time. You know, during the nightly news.

RON: What a Deity. Savior of the world and still manages to keep an eye on the Nielsen ratings during sweeps month.

PERRY: Well, Mr. "Who's Afraid of Final Judgment," I have assembled all the crucial data into my own self-published book, *Fifty Fun Facts for a Flame-proof Future.*

RON *(muttering):* Published by a fire retardant. *(To* PERRY*)* November 7, huh? When's the book come out?

PERRY: January.

RON: That could certainly hurt your royalty checks. Hope you got an advance up front.

PERRY: You don't believe in any of this, do you? The end of the world? Jesus returning? Final judgment?

RON: Sure, I do. But do I have to remind you about last week when you overheard the lady at the Stop 'N Shop say, "The king is coming"?

PERRY: How was I supposed to know she meant the Elvis impersonator at the Holiday Inn lounge?

RON: The next thing he knew he was surrounded by 300 people in white flight suits on Pogo sticks trying to get a head start on the Rapture.

PERRY *(defensive):* Hey, we were the biggest crowd he'd ever had. He did go ahead and sign all our Hal Lindsay books.

RON: Yeah, "Dear Perry, Return to Sender. The King." Funny guy.

PERRY: We'll see who gets the last laugh. I can't believe you haven't given one thought to that exact moment when time will stand still forever.

RON: You want to see time stand still, try to watch an hour of Congress on C-SPAN. Look Perry, here's the deal. Nobody knows, OK? Jesus said even He didn't know. So it's real simple to me. Number one, Jesus is coming back. Number two, it may be soon. Number three, I'd better be ready.

PERRY: That's it? I don't know . . .

RON: What's not to know? I think Jesus would much rather have me living my life full of His grace and forgiveness than poring over some obscure chart or standing around in a cave.

(While RON *continues talking* PERRY *leaves the cave the same way they entered, unbeknownst to* RON.*)*

RON *(continuing, shines his light on something in front of him):* Hey, would you look at that? There really is writing on the wall . . . I can't quite make it out . . . looks like . . . "No one knows . . . the time or the hour . . ." One of your little prophecy partners must have gotten in here ahead of us. *(Chuckles)*

Next thing you know, we'll find the words *(singing)*, "I wish we'd all been ready." Wouldn't that be the kicker, Perry? . . . Perry? . . . *(Looking around)* Perry!?

PERRY *(appearing again)*: Gotcha! *(Laughs)*

RON: Very funny.

PERRY: Come on, I guess you were right after all.

RON: So, you gonna finally give all this up?

PERRY: No, no, I mean about the coupon. They took it. Our pizza's up.

RON: Great . . . *(They start to leave.)*

PERRY: Come on, admit it. Just for a second, you wondered, didn't you?

RON: You know what the scariest thing about being left behind would be?

PERRY: Eternal damnation?

RON: Naw. Having to face Aunt Viola's flaming fajitas all alone.

(Blackout)